THE MINIAT

*H*ERBS

CRESCENT BOOKS
New York

Published by Salamander Books Limited
129-137 York Way, London N7 9LG, United Kingdom

© Salamander Books Ltd., 1991

This 1991 edition published by Crescent Books, distributed by
Outlet Book Company, Inc., a Random House Company,
225 Park Avenue South, New York, New York 10003.

Printed and bound in Belgium

ISBN 0-517-06109-0

87654321

CREDITS

RECIPES BY: *Judy Bastyra, Mary Cadogan, Julia Canning,
Kerenza Harries, Dolly Meers, Janice Murfitt, Cecilia Norman,
Lorna Rhodes, Sally Taylor, Carol Timperley and Mary Trewby*

PHOTOGRAPHY BY: *David Gill, Paul Grater, David Johnson,
Alan Newnham, Jon Stewart and Graham Tann*

DESIGN BY: *Tim Scott*

TYPESET BY: *The Old Mill*

COLOR SEPARATION BY: *P&W Graphics, Pte. Ltd.*

PRINTED IN BELGIUM BY: *Proost International Book Production,
Turnhout, Belgium*

$\mathcal{C}$ONTENTS

WATERCRESS SOUP WITH MARIGOLDS   8

GOATS' CHEESE WITH MINT   10

SMOKED SALMON PARCELS   12

HERBED BAKED EGGS   14

OYSTERS ROYALE   16

NEW ENGLAND CLAM CHOWDER   18

MUSTARD & TARRAGON-COATED LAMB   20

HICKORY SMOKED CHICKEN   22

PORK WITH HERBS   24

SMOKED FISH PLATTER   26

PASTA AND TAMARILLO SALAD   28

TRIO OF DIPS   30

CHICKEN & GRAPE SALAD   32

ASPARAGUS, HAM & CHICORY BITES   34

OATMEAL & HAM PANCAKES   36

HALOUMI & MINT LOAF   38

TRADITIONAL ALMOND BLANCMANGE   40

MINTED GRAPEFRUIT SORBET   42

TANGY LEMON MOLD   44

WATERCRESS SOUP
WITH MARIGOLDS

²⁄₃ cup garbanzo beans, soaked in cold water for 2 hours
3 thyme sprigs
3 tablespoons olive oil
1 leek, finely chopped
2 zucchini, cubed
1 carrot, sliced
2 tablespoons finely chopped parsley
4½ cups chicken stock
3 cups finely chopped watercress
Salt and pepper to taste
3 marigold flowers to garnish

*I*n a large saucepan, put beans and soaking liquid, thyme and enough water to cover by about 4 inches. Bring to a boil and boil steadily 10 minutes. Reduce heat, cover and simmer until beans are soft, about 30-40 minutes. Drain beans and discard thyme. In another pan, heat oil, add beans, leek, zucchini, carrot and parsley, and cook, covered, over low heat until vegetables soften, 10 minutes. Add stock and simmer until vegetables are tender, 15-20 minutes. Add watercress then puree pan contents until smooth. Reheat and season. If necessary, thin with a little chicken stock. Garnish with marigold petals. *Makes 4 servings.*

$\mathcal{G}$OATS' CHEESE
WITH MINT

⅓ cup milk

1 tablespoon olive oil

1 teaspoon lemon juice

6 oz goat cheese, sieved

½ red bell pepper, seeded, cut into thin strips

4 teaspoons chopped mint

Salt and pepper to taste

Mint sprigs to garnish

Crackers to serve, if desired

*I*n a bowl, beat milk, oil and lemon juice into goat cheese. Fold in red pepper strips and mint. Season to taste. Press mixture into 6 inch round dish. Cover and refrigerate at least 4 hours. To serve, garnish with mint spigs, and serve with crackers, if desired. *Makes 4 servings.*

SMOKED SALMON PARCELS

8 oz smoked salmon
2 (3-oz) pkgs. cream cheese, softened
2 tablespoons olive oil
2 teaspoons lime juice
3 tablespoons finely chopped dill weed
Black pepper to taste
4 teaspoons horseradish cream
Lime slices and dill sprigs to garnish

*L*ine 4 lightly oiled (⅓ cup) ramekin dishes with smoked salmon, leaving a little extra to cover the top. In a bowl, beat together cheese, oil and lime juice, then stir in dill, black pepper and any smoked salmon trimmings. Fold horseradish through, to distribute in strands. Divide mixture between ramekin dishes, cover with smoked salmon and refrigerate 3-4 hours. To serve, turn out onto individual small, cold plates and garnish with lime slices and dill sprigs. *Makes 4 servings.*

HERBED BAKED EGGS

4 thin slices ham
3 large eggs
1 teaspoon prepared mustard
¼ cup plain yogurt
2 teaspoons chopped fresh chives
2 teaspoons chopped fresh parsley
¾ cup shredded Cheddar cheese (3 oz)
Sprigs of herbs to garnish
Hot buttered toast to serve

*L*ine 4 greased ramekin dishes with ham. In a bowl, beat together eggs, yogurt and mustard. Mix together chives and parsley. Stir ½ of herb mixture and ¼ cup cheese into egg mixture. Spoon into ramekins and top with remaining cheese and herbs. Bake in an oven preheated to 375F (190C) until golden and set, about 25-30 minutes. To serve, turn out onto warm plates, garnish with sprigs of herbs and hand round hot buttered toast. *Makes 4 servings.*

OYSTERS ROYALE

48 oysters, cleaned
½ cup butter
2 tablespoons finely chopped green onion
2 teaspoons chopped fresh tarragon
1 teaspoon chopped fresh mint
1½ cups champagne
Salt and pepper, to taste
Mint sprigs to garnish
Toast to serve

To open oysters, place with flatter shell uppermost and hinge towards you, cover with a towel and insert the point of an oyster knife in gap in hinge. Twist blade to prize the shells open. Sever the muscle by sliding knife blade around the upper shell. Remove any chips of shell from the oyster. Set oysters aside; arrange 12 shells on each of 4 plates. In a saucepan, melt 2 tablespoons butter, add green onion, tarragon and mint and cook 1 minute. Add champagne, salt and pepper. Bring to a boil, then simmer to reduce liquid by ½. Gradually whisk in remaining butter to make a thick, creamy sauce.

Add oysters and heat gently 2 minutes. Spoon oysters into shells on plates, and cover them with a little sauce. Garnish with mint sprigs, and serve with toast. *Makes 4 servings.*

NEW ENGLAND
CLAM CHOWDER

2 (10-oz) cans clams
3 slices bacon, diced
1 medium-size onion, finely chopped
1 lb potatoes, diced
1 ¼ cups milk
1 ¼ cups fish stock
⅔ cup half and half
Pinch dried leaf thyme
Salt and pepper to taste

*D*rain clams; reserve liquid. Chop clams. In a large saucepan, fry bacon until fat runs and bacon is lightly browned. Add onion, cook until soft then stir in reserved clam liquid, potatoes, milk and stock. Bring to a boil, then simmer until potatoes are tender, about 20 minutes.

Stir in half and half, thyme, clams and salt and pepper. Heat gently for 2-3 minutes without boiling. *Makes 6 servings.*

$\mathcal{M}$USTARD &
TARRAGON-COATED LAMB

1 (4-lb) boneless lamb shoulder
2 garlic cloves, slivered
4 teaspoons dry mustard
2 teaspoons salt
Black pepper to taste
3 to 4 tarragon sprigs
1 tablespoon olive oil
2 tablespoons butter
1 onion, finely sliced
¾ cup white wine
1 tablespoon chopped tarragon
Sprigs of tarragon to garnish

*W*ith the point of a sharp knife, cut slits in the lamb. Insert garlic. Mix together mustard, salt and pepper. Spread ½ over inside of lamb, and place tarragon sprigs on top. Roll up and secure with string. Spread remaining mustard mixture over lamb. In a flameproof dish, heat oil and butter, add lamb and brown evenly. Add onions and cook until softened. Stir in wine. Cover and cook in oven preheated to 350F (175C) to required doneness, about 2½ to 3 hours. Pour fat off cooking juices. Simmer juices, stirring, for 2 to 3 minutes. Add chopped tarragon and pour into warmed jug. Cut string from lamb, and carve. Garnish with tarragon sprigs. *Makes 6-8 servings.*

HICKORY SMOKED CHICKEN

2 handfuls hickory smoking chip, soaked in hot water
Handful of mixed fresh herbs
1 (3- to 4-lb) broiler-fryer chicken
Salt to taste
Fresh flat-leaf parsley sprigs, radishes, cut in half, and lettuce
leaves to garnish

*H*eat a covered barbecue or wet smoker. Drain chicory chips and sprinkle over hot coals. Place a heatproof dish or pan of water over coals, and add herbs to water. Season chicken with salt, place on rack over dish or pan. Close barbecue cover. Reduce heat. Cook chicken over low coals, turning the bird every 30 minutes, until moist with slightly pink-tinged flesh and a characteristic smoky flavor, about 3 hours. Add water to water pan during cooking, if necessary by moving chicken out of the way and very carefully pouring in the water. Garnish with parsley, radishes and lettuce. *Makes 4-6 servings.*

$\mathcal{P}$ORK WITH HERBS

1 (1-lb) pork tenderloin, trimmed
1 tablespoon plus 1 teaspoon all-purpose flour
1 teaspoon half and half
MARINADE
2 tablespoons olive oil
1 tablespoon Madeira wine
½ teaspoon salt
½ teaspoon black pepper
1 teaspoon Dijon-style mustard
1 teaspoon superfine sugar
1 tablespoon grated onion
1 tablespoon chopped fresh sage
1 tablespoon chopped fresh oregano

*F*or the marinade, in a bowl, combine all marinade ingredients until evenly mixed. Lay pork in shallow baking dish, and pour marinade over, coating thoroughly. Cover and refrigerate 2 to 3 hours. Cook pork in oven preheated to 425F (220C) 15 minutes, basting once or twice with the marinade. Remove pork to a warm plate and keep warm. Stir flour into cooking juices then pour into a saucepan. Bring to a boil, stirring, and cook until thickened, about 2 minutes. Off the heat, stir in half and half. Cut pork into ½-thick slices and serve with the sauce. *Makes 4 servings.*

$\mathcal{S}$MOKED FISH PLATTER

2 smoked trout fillets, skinned
2 peppered smoked mackerel or smoked whitefish
fillets, skinned
2 tablespoons butter, room temperature
1 teaspoon lemon juice
3 slices firm-textured white bread, toasted
1 (3½-oz) can smoked oysters, drained
Small lettuce leaves of your choice
Lemon slices and fresh dill sprigs to garnish
HORSERADISH SAUCE
6 tablespoons plain yogurt
4 teaspoons prepared horseradish
2 teaspoons lemon juice
4 teaspoons chopped parsley
Black pepper to taste

*F*or the sauce, in a small bowl, mix all ingredients together well. Spoon into small serving dish. Cut trout into pieces; break mackerel or whitefish into pieces. In a small bowl, beat together butter and lemon juice. Using a small cookie cutter, cut 12 shapes from toast; spread with butter mixture and top each shape with a smoked oyster; arrange on 4 individual plates with fish pieces. Add lettuce leaves and garnish with lemon slices. Serve with sauce. *Makes 4 servings.*

$\mathcal{P}$ASTA & TAMARILLO SALAD

1 lb pasta shells
⅓ cup olive oil
3 tamarillos, peeled and thinly sliced
6 oz goat cheese, sliced or crumbled
DRESSING
½ cup olive oil
½ cup red-wine vinegar
2 garlic cloves, crushed
1 green bell pepper, seeded, chopped
1 small onion, chopped
1 (4-oz) can pimento, drained
3 tablespoons chopped parsley
3 tablespoons chopped basil
Salt and pepper to taste
Sprigs of basil to garnish

*I*n a large saucepan of boiling, salted water, cook pasta until just tender, about 8 to 10 minutes. Drain, rinse under warm water and drain well. Tip into a large bowl and toss with olive oil to coat thoroughly. Cover and refrigerate 30 minutes.

For the dressing, process all ingredients in a food processor or blender until smooth. Pour over pasta. Toss well. Add goat cheese and tamarillo, and toss carefully. Serve on individual plates, garnished with basil sprigs. *Makes 6 servings.*

TRIO OF DIPS

1¾ cup water
⅔ cup red lentils
2 garlic cloves
⅔ cup plain yogurt
1 (8-oz) pkg. cream cheese
2 tablespoons fromage frais
¼ cup chopped fresh mixed herbs
1 small eggplant
½ cup sour cream
1 tablespoon chopped fresh rosemary
Mixed vegetable sticks

*I*n a saucepan, bring water and lentils to a boil, then simmer until water has been absorbed and lentils are tender; cool. In a food processor or blender, process lentils with 1 garlic clove, and the yogurt until smooth. Season with salt and pepper. In a bowl, beat cream cheese, fromage frais and herbs together. Season with salt and pepper. Grill eggplant until skin is charred and flesh tender, turning occasionally. Cut in half, scoop out flesh into a food processor fitted with a steel blade, or blender; cool, then process with sour cream, remaining garlic and rosemary. Season with salt and pepper. Serve dips in serving bowls with selection of mixed vegetables. *Each dip makes 6-8 servings.*

CHICKEN & GRAPE SALAD

1 lb cold, cooked, boned chicken, diced
3 celery stalks, chopped
4 oz red grapes, halved, seeded if necessary
4 oz green grapes, halved, seeded if necessary
½ head lettuce of your choice, if desired, finely shredded
Whole grapes, nasturtium petals and fresh tarragon sprigs to
garnish
TARRAGON DRESSING
¼ cup virgin olive oil
4 teaspoons tarragon vinegar
¼ cup dairy sour cream
Salt and black pepper to taste

*I*n a medium-size bowl, combine chicken, celery and grapes.

For the dressing, in a small bowl, stir all ingredients together. Pour over salad; toss. Line 4 dinner plates with lettuce, if desired. Top with salad and garnish with whole grapes, nasturtium petals and fresh tarragon sprigs. *Makes 4 main-course servings.*

$\mathscr{A}$SPARAGUS, HAM & CHICORY BITES

8 oz asparagus spears, trimmed
3 heads chicory
1 (8-oz) pkg. cream cheese
3 slices proscuitto or parma ham
Tangerine wedges and dill sprigs to garnish
1 tangerine
½ clove garlic, crushed
¼ teaspoon salt
¼ teaspoon ground black pepper
½ teaspoon Dijon-style mustard
2 teaspoons honey
1 tablespoon plus 1 teaspoon olive oil
2 teaspoons chopped fresh tarragon

*H*alf-fill a shallow skillet with water, bring to a boil. Place asparagus in water and cook until tender, 3 to 4 minutes. Drain, place under cold running water to cool; drain. For the marinade, using a zester, remove tangerine peel in fine strips; reserve. Squeeze juice into a small bowl. Using a wooden spoon, stir in remaining ingredients. Pour over asparagus, cover and refrigerate 1 hour. Separate chicory leaves and cut in 1-inch slices. Spread with a little cream cheese. Cut asparagus in 1-inch slices; place on cream cheese. Wrap each with a ham strip. Garnish. *Makes 48 pieces.*

OATMEAL & HAM PANCAKES

½ cup all-purpose flour
⅓ cup regular rolled oats, ground
Pinch salt
6 large eggs, beaten
1¼ cups milk
2 tablespoons chopped fresh chives
8 thin slices smoked ham
2 tablespoons butter
1 to 2 tablespoons half and half
Salt and pepper to taste

In a bowl, sift together flour, oats and salt. Beat in 2 eggs, the milk and 1 tablespoon chives to form a smooth batter. Pour onto an oiled, hot griddle sufficient batter to make a 6-inch pancake. Cook 2 minutes, turn over, cook 1 minute then top with a slice of ham. Keep warm between 2 plates set over a pan of simmering water. Repeat until all the batter has been used.

In a small saucepan, melt butter, add remaining eggs and cook gently, stirring, until thickened. Off the heat, stir in half and half, remaining chives and salt and pepper. Place egg in center of each crepe, roll up and serve immediately. *Makes 8 servings.*

$\mathcal{H}$ALOUMI & MINT LOAF

1 (¼-oz) package active dried yeast (about 1 tablespoon),
dissolved in 1¼ cups warm water (110F/45C)
1¾ cups whole-wheat flour
2 cups all-purpose flour
1 teaspoon salt
1 tablespoon olive oil
3 tablespoons chopped mint
6 oz haloumi cheese, diced
1 tablespoon sesame seeds

*L*et yeast stand until frothy, about 5 minutes. In a large bowl, stir flours and salt together. Add remaining water and oil to yeast mixture, then gradually pour over flours, stirring, to make a smooth, soft dough. Knead until smooth and elastic. Place in a clean, lightly oiled bowl, cover and let rise until doubled in volume, about 1½ to 2 hours. Turn dough onto lightly floured surface. Punch down into a flattish round. Fold in cheese and mint and knead dough about 5 minutes. Form into an 8-inch round. Place on a floured baking sheet. Cut 1-inch from the edge, almost through to the bottom, all round. Brush top with water, and sprinkle with sesame seeds. Bake in an oven preheated to 450F (230C) 10 minutes; reduce temperature to 400F (205C) and continue baking about 20 minutes. Cool on a wire rack. *Makes 1 loaf.*

TRADITIONAL
ALMOND BLANCMANGE

½ cup whole blanched almonds
4 egg yolks
½ cup superfine sugar
1½ cups milk
3 tablespoons water
1 (¼-oz) envelope unflavored gelatin (1 tablespoon)
1 cup whipping cream, lightly whipped
Toasted sliced almonds and fresh herbs to decorate, if desired

*P*lace almonds under preheated grill, turning frequently until evenly browned. Cool. In a food processor fitted with a metal blade, or blender, grind coarsely. Beat egg yolks and sugar until thick and light. In a saucepan, heat milk almost to boiling point; stir into egg mixture. Pour back into rinsed pan and cook over low heat, stirring, until thick enough to coat the back of the spoon; do not boil. Strain into bowl and cool. Add water to a small bowl, sprinkle gelatin over and let stand until softened, 2 to 3 minutes. Set bowl over saucepan of hot water and stir until dissolved. Stir into milk mixture and let stand until just at setting point. Stir in prepared almonds, then fold in cream. Spoon into a decorative dish, or individual dishes. Refrigerate until set. Sprinkle with toasted sliced almonds and chopped herbs, if desired. *Makes 6 servings.*

$\mathcal{M}$INTED GRAPEFRUIT SORBET

¾ cup superfine sugar
½ cup water
Juice of 2 grapefruit
Juice of 1 lime
1 tablespoon finely chopped mint leaves
2 egg whites
3 kiwifruit
Sprigs of mint to decorate

*I*n a saucepan, gently heat sugar in water until dissolved, then boil 5 minutes. Pour into a bowl; cool. Strain in grapefruit and lime juices, and add mint. Pour into freezerproof container, cover and freeze until half-frozen, about 2 to 3 hours. Spoon into cold bowl. Whip egg whites to form stiff peaks. Fold into half-frozen mixture. Return to container, cover and freeze until just firm. Turn into cold bowl, beat until smooth, then freeze until required. To serve, puree kiwifruit and pour over 4 dessert plates. Using 2 dessert spoons, scoop out ovals of sorbet and arrange 3 on each plate. Decorate with mint sprigs. *Makes 4 servings.*

TANGY LEMON MOLD

3 small egg yolks
2½ cups milk
⅓ cup granulated sugar
1 (¼ oz) envelope unflavored gelatin (1 tablespoon)
Grated peel and juice of 1 large lemon
⅔ cup superfine sugar
Twists of lemon and fresh herbs to garnish, if desired

*I*n a bowl, lightly beat egg yolks. In a saucepan, stir together milk, granulated sugar and gelatin. Over low heat, stirring, bring almost to boiling point. Slowly stir into egg yolks. Pour into a 3¾-cup mold, cool, then refrigerate until set. Meanwhile, in a small saucepan, stir together lemon peel and juice and superfine sugar. Place over low heat and stir until sugar dissolves; cool. To serve, turn out mold onto cold plate. Pour lemon sauce around and decorate with lemon twists and fresh herbs, if desired. *Makes 4 servings.*